Hear His Voice

BY MICHAEL J. LUSARDI

CREATION
HOUSE
PRESS

HEAR HIS VOICE by Michael J. Lusardi
Published by Creation House Press
A Part of Strang Communications Company
600 Rinehart Road
Lake Mary, FL 32746
www. creationhouse.com

Library of Congress Control Number: 2001093483
International Standard Book Number: 0-88419-795-6

01 02 03 04 05 – 7 6 5 4 3 2 1

Printed in the United States of America

DEDICATION

This book is dedicated to the following people who have played such a tremendous role in my life. Their lifestyles truly exemplify what it means to live a spirit-filled, uncompromising, and sold-out life for Jesus Christ.

To my parents, Dr. and Mrs. Philip T. Lusardi, I would like to say, "thank you for all your prayers and support. You both are the 'unsung' heroes in my life. May I bring you some of the joy that you have brought my life—I love you both!"

Paula da Rosa, thank you for the encouragement and guidance, and for opening your home to me during the difficult times in my life. I bless God for your life.

Debra Keena, what an inspiration you are. You are truly an example of someone who is *totally* sold-out for Jesus Christ. Thank you for your "listening ear" when I just needed to "vent." I also want to thank you for putting the fire under me to get this book finished—with a spirit of excellence. *"Look, I did it!"*

Grace Muñoz and Sherry Carpenter, you both have been a blessing to me. You are two women so in tune with the Holy Spirit. Thank you for your prayers, support, teaching and, yes, correction—Oh, the correction. I have appreciated your honesty over the years.

To my associate in ministry and best friend, Wayne Schmidt, I would like to say, "Thank you, for being the 'backbone' of this project. Your encouragement, faith and push to get this book published was the answer to much prayer and was a 'wake-up' call. You are a blessing! I am blessed to call you *friend.*"

TABLE OF CONTENTS

FOREWORD

God desires to communicate with His children. Jesus Christ's sacrifice on the cross at Calvary guarantees Christians a direct line of communication with our Father. If you desire to truly *hear His voice*, author and pastor Michael J. Lusardi's compilation of inspirational conversations with his Lord will renew your faith and hope in God.

The letters contained in *Hear His Voice* will encourage Christians of all ages to seek the wisdom, knowledge and discernment with which our Father longs to bless us! The following pages reflect the love, compassion and insight that the Father has shown Michael on a daily basis. I invite you to seek out your blessing as the Father reveals Himself to you in the pages of this book.

WAYNE L. SCHMIDT
CO-FOUNDER, SALVATION HOUSE
SAN DIEGO, CA

PREFACE

One morning I sat down to do my daily devotional. It appeared as if it would be like any other day. Don't get me wrong, these times of fellowship are a blessing, and they are filled with extreme fulfillment. However, this time it was different; God had something *special* for me—something that would go beyond the area of personal prayer, reading and study. God wanted me, not only to hear Him speak in the quietness, but to hear His *voice and tell others what He is saying.*

Often, we come into our "prayer closet" and ramble off. What do I mean? We present our "grocery list" to Him. *I want—I need—God, I am in need of...*and so goes the story. But how often do we seek His face and not merely His hands? How often do we just tell Him how good He is? "Lord, You are good! I just want to give *You* something today." What a switch! To position yourself in a place of blessing—to bless *Him*. If we seek His face, by the time we realize it, not only His hands, but His arms are already wrapped around us.

It requires little or no effort to seek Him when we are in need or we're in the eye of the storm, but how much effort does it take to seek Him during the calm? For some that is a battle in itself. "The spirit is willing, but the flesh is weak." Oh, how weak it really is. To paraphrase the apostle Paul, "I do those things that I don't want to do, and don't do what I ought to do."

This particular morning was different. God spoke just as He had before, but this time with much greater passion, love and fervor. He moved on me, and I picked up a pen and began to write. As I began writing, I realized that I was no longer in control. I was not in control of my words, my pen or my hand. I was simply His vessel taking dictation. I watched in amazement as my hand moved across the page yet my mind did not know what would come next. Yes, the words filled the paper, but I had to read what I was writing or I would have no awareness as to what was being written. I know that may be difficult to understand. I myself did not. I even wrote words of which I did not know the meanings. But when I later looked them up in the dictionary, I was even more amazed to see just how accurately placed they were. To God be the glory!

Hear His Voice is a collection of personal letters filled with words that I strongly believe the Lord has impressed upon my heart to write on paper. This is merely one way of attempting to understand the love, mercy, and compassion He feels toward His children. Each letter is written from an individualistic perspective and intended to impact each reader differently—yet the same.

When you praise and worship our Lord and acknowledge His presence, you surrender to His will. Upon surrendering, you become sensitive enough to be led by His Spirit. In those quiet times of waiting upon Him, you can hear a small still voice coming from the depths of your heart.

This book is meant to be an added encouragement to the reader by giving a close, sensitive and personal perspective of daily struggles and victories one may encounter on one's journey.

I pray these words will encourage you as much as they have encouraged me. Though I, myself, may not have gone through some of these experiences, I believe the anointing of the Holy Spirit has allowed me to share in the emotions surrounding each experience.

When there is little hope, God will always give us the faith and the strength to go on. His love and mercy truly endure forever. During those quiet times before Him, my prayer for you is that you, too, may *hear His voice*.

ACKNOWLEDGMENTS

First and foremost, I would like to thank our heavenly Father for demonstrating the most pure and unselfish act of love that will ever be known to man. He loves us so much, that He sent His only Son to redeem us. The gift of His Son truly exemplifies undying and unselfish love to its extremes.

I would also thank my personal Savior, Jesus Christ. Though You made me a writer, how can I even begin to express in words what You have done to and for me? Jesus, You have given me hope which I have never known before. Better yet, You have given me *faith*. My Lord, You gave Yourself up for me as a sacrifice. I am forever grateful to You! I love You with all my heart, mind and soul!

Even when I turned my back on You, You still were there waiting patiently for my return. Jesus, I thank You that even when I was unfaithful, You always remained faithful. I thank You for the opportunity to come to You in repentance, knowing that You are faithful and just to forgive me and cleanse me from all unrighteousness.

Holy Spirit, I thank You for all the fellowship that You orchestrate between my Creator, my Savior and me. It is Your power and presence that has strengthened and encouraged me during the most difficult times of my life. Thank You for allowing me to *hear Your voice*.

WORDS TO LIVE BY...

With Jesus, you always get a second chance to *make a first impression.*

His Eyes Are on the Sparrow

*M*y child,

I know you feel as if you are not appreciated, but consider My Son, Jesus. He was despised and rejected by His own people. Strive not to please the hearts of men, but you must live in the Truth; that is, the knowledge of My Son that set you free. Truth that has set you free from *every* form of bondage—*including* the need for acceptance of others.

Do not compromise your walk by attempting to please man. My child, I see your service; you are not *unnoticed* by Me. You have humbled yourself in service before Me, and your work is not in vain. *In due season* I will raise you up. I will mount you up on eagle's wings. You will feel the freedom of My love brush against you. I will strengthen you in times of need. For in your weakness I shall make you strong.

You are one of My prized possessions—did you know that? Well, you certainly are! I am so proud of you. Even if you think no one takes notice of you, I do. And I love you!

Your Father

Suggested Reading:

Proverbs 16:33; John 9:4; 1 Corinthians 15:58; Colossians 3:23-24; Hebrews 6:10-12; James 4:10

EVERY VALLEY RAISED—EVERY MOUNTAIN LOWERED

*M*y child,

There are so many areas in your life in which I have already begun to work. When I see you, I see a finished work. Be patient, little one. I have only begun to show you the advantages of serving Me. I know it can be difficult at times. Perhaps, at times, you do not even *feel* My presence. However, I tell you this day not to be moved by *feelings*, but *faith*.

Child, I have never left your side. I know you do not understand why certain situations occur in your life. One thing is for sure: if you learn to cast all your cares upon Me through the trials, I will strengthen you and give you grace through them all.

Sometimes, when you are in the valleys, you may think that there is no way out. However, only until you have climbed those mountains in your life will you be able to look down at those valleys and understand their reason for existing. At an *appointed* time, you will even *appreciate* them, for you will have grown in the midst of them.

Lean not to your own understanding. You limit what I am able to do when you walk by sight rather than by faith. Remember, little one, My ways are not your ways. I know what is best for you—be patient.

Your Father

Suggested Reading:

Proverbs 3:5; 2 Corinthians 12:9-10; James 1:2-11; 1 Peter 5:7

A Surrendered Heart

*M*y child,

Surrendering your will to Me is not always an easy thing to do. It does take faith on your part; however, part of faith is trusting. How can you trust someone you do not really know? Little one, how I long for your fellowship! I enjoy the moments that we share. Those moments of *total* surrender allow Me to be the center of your existence.

Did you know that, when you praise Me, you allow Me to become the very thing for which you praise Me? Sometimes I will even drop subtle hints to remind you of My presence in your life. When you *choose* to take notice—how My heart leaps for joy!

Did you know that I rejoice over you with singing? Well, I do! You are My prized possession; I take care of those things that belong to Me.

That is why it is important for you to have a *surrendered* heart. A surrendered heart unto Me shall never lose its way. For in everything you do, I have gone before you. Walk in My light. These blessings that you are *beginning* to tread upon are just a glimpse of what is to come. Be patient, little one.

Your Father

Suggested Reading:

Proverbs 3:5; Zephaniah 3:17; John 14:1; 2 Corinthians 6:11-13

The Father Knows How to Keep Time

My child,

How many times do I have to tell you to trust Me? I am at work; wait and see My goodness. You have not received what you have asked of Me because I desire to give you much more.

I am waiting for the *right* moment to bless you. You have to understand that timing is everything. When I give, it has to be the right *time*, the right *blessing* to give and for all the right *reasons*. I am considering your welfare.

You would only be able to withstand My blessings a little at a time. Yes, too much of a good thing without the character has *wasteful* potential. Does a mother give more milk than her baby is able to withstand? Of course not, her child would choke. She feeds her child in moderation. I AM the God of balance. Little one, I am only giving what *you* are able to handle. Be patient—My blessings await *you*!

Your Father

Suggested Reading:

Proverbs 20:21; Isaiah 30:18; Ezekiel 34:26-31; Malachi 3:10; Colossians 1:10-14

THE MUSTARD SEED PRINCIPLE

*M*y child,

When I said that without faith it was impossible to please Me, consider My reasoning. First of all, *faith* is being sure of what is hoped for and being certain that I will bring it to pass—regardless of what you can or cannot see. If you come to Me, you must believe that I exist and am more than able to reward those who seek Me *diligently*.

If you had leaned to your own understanding, you would have never come to know Me. It is by *faith* that you accepted Me into your heart and by *faith* you are saved. It is by My grace, not by works. If it had been by works, you would have never come to the place of total surrender.

Learn to cast all your cares upon Me, for I care for you. I am interested in everything that pertains to you. I created you, and you are *fearfully* and *wonderfully* made. I would not have settled for anything less.

Let Me ask you this: Would you trust a perfect stranger? Certainly not. Trust and faith are the same. You cannot have one without the other. How can you have *faith* in someone you do not know and trust? You must learn to hear My voice and seek My face. The more you get to know Me, the more you will be able to trust Me. I promise that I will not let you down!

P.S. All the *faith* you need is the size of a mustard seed. Consider the mustard seed, the smallest of all seeds; yet, when grown to its full maturity, it becomes the largest of all.

Your Father

Suggested Reading:

Hebrews 11:1, 6; Matthew 9:27-29; 17:20-21

✝

SALVATION—THE GREATEST GIFT

*M*y child,

Happiness is not in how educated you are, how much money you make, or who your friends are. You can search all your life for happiness in these things; however, you will *never* find it.

You ask why? The reason is because I created you that way. You may be able to find *temporary* gratification in materialistic possessions, popularity and intellect. However, you will *always* desire, to the point of unrest, more money, more friends and more knowledge.

Little one, if you do not allow Me access into your life, you will *never* truly be fulfilled. When I created you, I made a *special* place in your heart in which *only* I can take residence and fill the void.

My love is the only thing that will truly satisfy you. However, I will never force Myself on you. I wait, patiently, outside the door of your heart, knocking. Sometimes, I will even allow all your options in life to be taken so you will look to Me for direction.

I stand in line behind all that you desire. My child, delight yourself in Me, and I *will* give you the desires of your heart. I will give happiness in its pureness and *without* worry or heaviness.

Your Father

Suggested Reading:

1 Samuel 16:7; Psalm 37:4-5; Revelation 3:20

I Will Never Leave You

*M*y child,

How long must you continue to look to your past failures? Must I remind you that you are a *new* creation in My Son? I have *removed* all transgressions from you, as far as the east is from the west. I have hurled them into the depths of the sea.

As My Son died, so must you. You must die to yourself so that you may share in His resurrection. That death also includes the death to your shame, guilt and fears. You must remember that you are enabled to do all things, for I will strengthen you in your time of need. However, I require that you make no provisions for failure. Learn to receive My grace and the liberty it brings.

Those times you feel defeated or feel that I am distant, know that I am there. Every parent must allow his or her child to grow. I am giving you that time to mature and develop character. When you feel like giving up, remember that in your weakness My strength will be made perfect. I will make you strong and give you the grace to endure.

P.S. Those times that you feel My absence, little one, I am *still*. It is during those times that I am at work the most. I reassure you of that.

Your Father

Suggested Reading:

Psalm 32:1; 103:12; 2 Corinthians 12:9; Philippians 3:14

Faith Requires Exercise

*M*y child,

Why must you continue to live in fear? I have not given you a spirit of fear but of *power, love* and a sound, *self-disciplined* mind. In everything you do, I go before you. If I go before you, who can be against you?

I would never give you anything that you are not able to handle. The devil will come to steal, kill and destroy. However, I have come to give you life—abundant life. I know sometimes you question why I allow him to do certain things. But look at it this way—you have become stronger through it all. In order for strength to be built up, by natural law, there has to be some form of resistance. Are you beginning to understand, now?

You *must* exercise faith to overcome. Faith can only come from *understanding, believing* and *applying* My Word. I know your strengths and your weaknesses. Remember, I know your past—*all is forgiven*. I know your present, and I know a factor you do not—I know your future. Trust Me, child, I will never leave you or forsake you.

I will always complete that which I have started. I never do anything halfway. When I open a door for you, you can be sure that what you find will already have been done by Me.

P.S. For every door that I close in your life, another will I open.

Your Father

Suggested Reading:

1 Corinthians 16:9; 2 Corinthians 12:9-10; Colossians 4:3; Acts 14:27; Romans 8:28-39

Be Thou Loosed—But Let Go!

*M*y child,

Do you honestly think that being dependent upon a substance is My will for your life? Of course not! I saved you to be free from all the chains that once had you bound. My anointing upon your life shall destroy the yoke of *every* bondage—if you let it. I gave you the power of My Spirit so that you could be an overcomer.

The only thing I want you to be dependent upon is My love for you. My love is untainted and life giving. If something alters the way you think, feel or act, contrary to My ways, it controls you. You do not control it.

It is not My desire for you to harm your body. I want your body to be a clean and pure-living sacrifice unto Me. It is then, that My holiness can surround you. My life will flow from within you.

Please do not be deceived into thinking that you control it. It already controls *you*. If you controlled it, it would not have been part of your life for this long. I know it is not an easy thing to let go of; allow Me to help you. I have made you more than a conqueror! My love has made sure of that.

P.S. Whatever you give up for My namesake, you will receive a hundred times more in this life, *and* you will inherit eternal life. Submit yourself to My will and purpose, and upon resisting the devil and his temptations, he must flee from you! There is no other *option* left to him!

Your Father

Suggested Reading:

James 4:7-8; Romans 8:35-39; 12:1-2; Proverbs 23:19-21

IRON AGAINST IRON

*M*y child,

I know it can sometimes be difficult to get along with everyone, but, little one, humble yourself. There is none perfect, not even you. Everyone has shortcomings. And, in all honesty, you have your fair share.

At times, the shortcomings are so hidden that you do not even realize they are there. You may have even grown accustomed to them; however, child, I have not. I have allowed them to surface, now, in order to humble you. I do not want you to be full of pride, for, if pride engulfs you, you *shall* fall!

Now and then, I will send someone in your path to deal with those areas. Little one, they shall be the sand in your life. You are bound to feel some irritation.

Look at the oyster, for instance. When sand finds its way inside the shell, the sand will irritate the oyster, forming a pearl. Look at the diamond; it is the finished product of extreme heat, pressure and fine "cutting" workmanship—the more precise the cut, the greater the brilliance. I want My light to penetrate and illuminate through you—without cloudiness or dullness.

I want to make something beautiful of your life. However, pride and self-righteousness hinder My work. You **must** humble yourself. And in due season, I will raise you up.

Your Father

Suggested Reading:

Romans 3:9-18; 12:1-21; 15:1-6; Colossians 3:5-17

✝

UNDYING LOVE

My child,

I have been with you since before you were born. I knew your name before you entered your mother's womb. I know your every thought. I also know that your love for Me is great, but My love for you is greater—so much that I died for your salvation.

Even though you turn away, I will always take you back. My love for you will never die, even if your faith in Me dies. My faith in you will live until the end of time.

My love for you is a neverending flame. No matter how hard anyone blows, it will not flicker. The inspiration of My Holy Spirit is much greater than that of evil. Nothing shall ever separate you from My love.

Your Father

Suggested Reading:

Deuteronomy 30; Psalm 139; Jeremiah 1:4-5a; 3:12-25; 4:1-4; Ezekiel 37:27-28; Romans 8:37-39

An Empty Canvas

*M*y child,

Have I not brought you this far? Do you think that I would honestly bring you this far to leave you destitute? Come now, child, I am always with you. Part of walking by faith is believing *without* seeing, is it not?

Your life is an empty canvas—My Son's blood made sure of that. I am an *Artist*. I made you, did I not? My Spirit is the *Paintbrush*. An unfinished painting never looks like a masterpiece for the reason that it is *unfinished*. However, when it is complete and you gaze upon its beauty, you would have never imagined that it could become so beautiful. Especially while it was in the process of being painted.

You are merely in the "process" stage. Be reassured, little one, you have only "pencil-sketched" an outline. I am *allowing* room for mistakes. Your mistakes, I can *always* erase.

Your Father

Suggested Reading:

Hebrews 12:2; 1 John 1:9; 2 Corinthians 5:7; Proverbs 3:5-6

Uncompromised Freedom

*M*y child,

How many times do I have to tell you that *obedience* is better than sacrifice? Obeying My voice, pleases Me far more than sacrifice. Sacrifice may *satisfy* your guilty conscience, but it does not please Me.

Little one, My desire is not to discourage you but to strengthen and encourage you. I do not give you laws to inhibit you but to *protect* you.

I do not try to trap you and then put you into a cage. I have redeemed you, child. You are *now* finally free! Consider My laws as protection from the outside. What would happen if I put you in this world all by yourself, without regulations? The cares of this world would surely devour you!

I have separated you and called you out by name! A costly *price* has been paid for you. All I ask in return is your love and obedience. Remember this: I am your *Hiding Place*. I will protect you from trouble and surround you with songs of deliverance—I promise.

Your Father

Suggested Reading:

Exodus 20; Joshua 22:5; 1 Samuel 15:22-23, Proverbs 2; Hebrews 13:17

Come Out From Among Them

My y child,

As any parent would, I desire the best for My children. I am only thinking of *your* welfare. I trust you in making decisions. You chose to accept the gift of My salvation, did you not? However, I am concerned with the company that you choose to keep. I have a deep and genuine concern for you, little one.

I am not trying to cut you off from life's existence, but I do not want you to get hurt either. Of the road you are on, pain will be the end result. It is inevitable; I assure you. I want to spare you all the unnecessary hurt.

Continue following this path of destruction, and, later, you will ask Me why it is happening to you. You will question *Me* for allowing such a thing to happen.

Child, if you will hear and obey My warning, by paying attention to the caution signs that I am placing before you, you will spare yourself all *unnecessary* pain.

When I created you (and I remind you that you are fearfully and wonderfully made), I created you with a free will to choose. Please do not misuse that freedom. You must live with every choice that you make.

You may choose the world, filled with its empty promises of fulfillment. Yes, it has the fast, upbeat pace of life with glamour, prestige and enticing benefits. However, it will ultimately lead to death and destruction. On the other hand, you can choose to follow Me. My promises are fulfilled, and the pace all depends on you and your willingness. You also benefit in sharing in My glory, which leads to abundant life. The choice is yours! Choose wisely!

If you choose to follow Me, you will find yourself doing and seeing things that you never dreamed possible. Child, I make all things possible, for I AM the God of possibilities. I am *able* to do exceedingly, abundantly above all you may ask or think, for I AM God! I stand alone and without limit!

P.S. The job to follow Me may be hard work, with limited time off, no vacations, and low pay, but the benefits are truly out of this world!

Your Father

Suggested Reading:

Deuteronomy 30:1; Isaiah 48:16-18; John 15:3; 2 Corinthians 6:14-18; 7:1

✝

Dear Father,

There are so many times that I do not feel Your presence in my life. There also have been times that You have told me that I am not to be moved by my feelings but by faith.

Father, rather than act out of emotion, my prayer is for You to help me to walk by faith and not by sight. Lord, teach me to trust in You and to wait upon You.

After all, You taught me to walk thus far. What I see is only temporary, and what I cannot see is eternal. Lord, help me not to put temporary value on what is eternal. Remind me that those times when I do not feel Your presence are the times when You are at work the most!

Gratefully,

_____

LEARNING TO WALK—EVERY DAY

*M*y child,

Promotions come from Me and not man. I have chosen to put you in this place of position to mature you. No man can come against My will for your life. Remain in My will, child.

You are beginning to *learn* to walk in My light. *Knowledge*, in all capacities, will lead to *responsibility* and some form of discipline on the part of the one who learns. You must walk in that knowledge of truth, which has set you free.

Being a vessel of My glory means knowing *who* is in control. I would not give you anything that I thought you were not able to withstand. Occasionally, you will get knocked down, and that is all right. However, I have given you the power, through My Spirit, to get up and fight the good fight.

I will never leave your side. Seek My face, child, and wait on Me. Learn to hear My voice, for My words will point you to a broad spectrum of strategies that are *not* subject to failure.

P.S. No weapon formed against you will prosper. You have My Word, and I am not man that I should have any reason to lie to you.

Your Father

Suggested Reading:

Psalm 1; Proverbs 12:1-2; Isaiah 30:20-21; 2 Corinthians 4:6; 1 John 1:7

THE COMFORT IS IN KNOWING

*M*y child,

Trust in Me, little one. I am working in your life. I know there are times that you question what I allow to occur in your life. I am the *Author* and *Finisher* of your faith, am I not? I allow circumstances to happen in your life for reasons that I will choose to reveal at a later time—an *appointed* time.

I allow certain incidents to happen in order to bring you closer to Me. Not only will they bring you into My presence where you will find peace, but they will strengthen you as well. Child, you are in training. **You will get through this**, trust Me.

Remember this: Others will find comfort in knowing that you understand, because you have shared in the same pain that they are experiencing. You asked to do My will and to see others through My eyes with the same compassion. It is necessary for you to go through similar experiences. This is the only way to understand the pain of My children.

Rejoice in Me, always. Did you know that I rejoice in you? Well, I do. You have come a long way, child. I am proud of you!

Your Father

Suggested Reading:

Isaiah 40; Galatians 6; Hebrews 12:2

A Brand-New Day

*M*y child,

Precious, little one, you must *continue* to walk in My light. I shall lead your every step. A heart surrendered unto Me shall never lose its way. Your heart belongs to Me. I shall never lose or misplace My most valuable possessions. Yes, I will remind you of this truth.

Search My heart for the answer that you have been waiting to hear. If you listen long enough, you may hear My gentle voice within the quietness. In all circumstances, praise Me, child. You cannot even begin to realize how much power is released when you do so.

In praising Me, you *allow* Me to give you grace through your turmoil. My desire is not to see you hurting; My desire is to see you joyous. This is My joy: to share in your happiness.

I know your *present* situation *appears* to be unbearable, but look back at your previous battles. You won them victoriously, did you not? I won each one of them before they ever began.

Trust Me, little one. Your sorrow may last through the night, but joy will come in the morning!

Your Father

Suggested Reading:

2 Chronicles 20; Proverbs 4:4; 10-12; 20-23

KEEP YOUR EYES ON ME

*M*y child,

Sometimes, words will not suffice. Listen with your heart, child, and not your mind. Open your heart to what My Spirit is telling you. If you listen long enough, you can hear *My* voice.

Many people will give their opinions and their perspectives, but you have chosen to listen to Me. My child, I have heard your cry in your darkest hour. No one but Me knows your *secret* pain. You must continue to look to Me and cast all your cares upon Me. I will honor the trust that you have in Me. Cast those burdens on Me, and allow Me to carry the load for you.

Have faith in Me. Faith will come by hearing My Word, and it will cast out all doubt.

You must remember that a decision made during distress or an emotional time will most likely be the wrong decision. Remain where I have placed you—for now. Keep your eyes focused on Me and not man. Pass no judgments and make no decisions based upon the frailty of man. You must look to Me.

If I choose to move you on, it will be a decision that *I* will make, regardless of what anyone else has to say. You will know when *I* have made that decision. I will

give you inner peace, gracing you through those doors
that I have opened for you—even when others attempt
to close them.

Your Father

Suggested Reading:

Deuteronomy 4:29-30; Proverbs 4:23-27; Hebrews 12

Forgiving Is Forgetting

*M*y child,

Owe no man anything, but love one another; for he that loves another has filled the law.

Not only do I want you to be out of debt financially, but spiritually as well. Do not harbor resentment and unforgiveness deep within your heart!

My greatest commandment to you is to love Me with all your heart, mind and soul. My second command is as the first: Love your neighbor as yourself. For when you love Me, you will always share the love that I have for others.

Owe no man forgiveness, for forgiveness is given unsparingly by Me. As freely as I give, it is *expected* for you to do the same. I say unto you that if you confess your sins before Me, I am faithful to show you My forgiveness. I will cleanse you of all unrighteousness.

Forgiveness and love I give unto you. I give to you so that you will *give* to others. Release all offenses to Me. They will only continue to hurt you if you bury them in your heart. They will, eventually, slow My work. Place them at My feet, child. I promise to bring forth healing. *Share the gift of forgiveness that you have been given so graciously.*

Your Father

Suggested Reading:

Matthew 6:14-15; John 13:34-35; Acts 13:37-39; Ephesians 4:29-32; 1 John 1:9

Of No Reputation

*M*y child,

Man cannot curse what I have blessed. I have blessed you abundantly. Take heed to *My* words, for I am God and not man that I should lie. My concern for you lies within the depths of your soul.

Little one, *where* you choose to worship Me is of no concern to Me if you are at peace. I cannot be contained within an image nor within the confinement of four walls. I brought you to where you are now, and I will be the One to move you—rest in Me. When I choose to move you on, you will know.

Child, how it burdens Me to tell you this, but not *everyone* welcomes the idea of your *departure*. However, you must ask yourself, *Am I fulfilling God's will for my life?* I am far more pleased when you are obedient to My calling and not wasting time on those who will never receive you or who challenge you at every point.

Remember, child, I am omnipresent. My house shall be made of those who are in agreement, standing as a body of believers in unity. For a house divided against itself cannot remain standing. I will always inhabit the *pure* praises of those who humble themselves before

Me. If your desire is to do My will, how can I not honor you for that? I honor your desire to please Me. Many people will come to discourage or *oppose* you. Unfortunately, it is expected. However, stand fast, for no weapon formed against you shall prosper. Remain in My will, and I shall hide you under the shadow of My wings. Rejoice!

P.S. Be strengthened! I am far more pleased when you act upon what you believe I am telling you to do. Upon doing this, you conquer the fear of your reputation being affected. Just a reminder—I did make Myself of no reputation.

Your Father

Suggested Reading:

Numbers 23-24; Revelation 3:8-12

SERVANTHOOD, NOT HOLLYWOOD

*M*y child,

How often must I remind you to just be yourself? You cannot please everyone. I am far more interested in your *originality* than your ability to conform to the ways of man. Just be yourself!

Your days of being someone you are not and trying to impress everyone are now over. So stop living in the minds of others! Tuck this deep within your spirit; My Son, in all His humility, was the Servant of all. When He washed the feet of His disciples, He humbly demonstrated servanthood.

Your desire should be similar. You are to have the heart of a servant, but *not* a slave, unto man. Servanthood— that is My heart! I want you to see others through My eyes. I see love, mercy and compassion. Judge not others so that you may not be judged.

This is neither a popularity contest nor a political campaign. Rid yourself of *selfish* agendas. Little one, do not criticize your brothers and sisters with the time you waste bickering amongst yourselves, you could be winning souls rather than crushing them. Put that extra energy into working the harvest. The harvest is plenty, but the workers are so few—*so quit trying to get rid of them!*

Work together in one mind and one accord. I desire My children to be united for My cause. This *should* be your cause as well. Keep your eyes upon Me, for I, and I alone, am the *Author* and *Perfector* of your faith.

Your Father

Suggested Reading:

Psalm 133:1; Proverbs 3:11-12; 24:28-29; Matthew 7:1-27; 1 Corinthians 3:5-11; Colossians 3:23-25

My sheep listen to my voice;
I know them, and
they follow me.
—John 10:27

HASTE MAKES WASTE

*M*y child,

Who is calling the shots here? You have asked for what you believed was My will, yet you have acted upon *your* own volition. When you asked Me, you asked Me in faith, believing that I had the ability.

Little one, I do. However, I have chosen to do matters *My* way and in My own time. That does not mean that it will never come to pass. Do not rush what I am doing. In doing so, you put Me in a difficult position—not for Me, but you. You leave Me no other alternative but to *allow* the consequences to fall upon your life.

You will find yourself left in doubt and confusion. This is not My will for your life. The end result will be quite devastating.

You have put yourself in a position that suggests I am incapable of taking care of matters. I am more than able to finish that which I have started. You have taken matters into your own hands, tying Mine. Child, I am more than able. I can do all things—for am I not the God who created all things? *I AM!*

Lean not to your own understanding. Look not to what your eyes see but what My Spirit is telling you. Be encouraged. It is not by your power and might. Allow My Holy Spirit access to work in your life!

Your Father

Suggested Reading:

Psalm 138:8; Proverbs 3:5-6; Romans 4:18-24; 8:24-27; Ephesians 3:20; Colossians 1:5-12

WORDS CREATE

*M*y child,

Sometimes, it is far better to listen than to speak. Far more knowledge is obtained by listening rather than by speaking. *Be quick to listen and slow to speak.* For within your mouth lies the power to give *life* or *death*.

There are many times that I would rather you remain silent. In doing so, you will be able to hear *My* voice and allow Me to speak for you. This is to *your* advantage, I assure you.

I did not give you a mouth to never speak. However, I do not want you to be ignorant of what I am telling you. The tongue can be a dangerous weapon if it is not used with caution and discipline. *Choose your words wisely.*

Let *My* words flow from your mouth, for *My* Word is truth. It is that truth that has set you free and will keep you holy unto Me. Give not yourself over, as a slave, to a gossiping tongue nor be associated with those who do. In case you have forgotten, what does light have to do with darkness, anyway? Separate yourself from all unholiness. Your reward will be great, let Me assure you!

Your Father

Suggested Reading:

Psalm 34:11-22; 39:1-5; Proverbs 13:3; James 1:19-26; 1 Peter 3:10

✝

WORDS TO LIVE BY...

A sanctified imagination gives birth to and *houses Godly vision.*

THERE IS A SEASON FOR EVERYTHING

*M*y child,

There is a season for everything. There is a time to laugh, a time to cry, a time to live and a time to die. Though seasons may change, one fact remains: My love *never* changes. My love stays the same—yesterday, today and forever.

My love may be unconditional; however, My promises of blessing are *conditional.* My love reaches the unreachable, but My promises of blessing *only* reach those who seek My face. Those who seek My face truly know Me and know My will. They will inherit all that I have promised.

Little one, I desire to fulfill those promises in your life. However, seeking Me *only* in times of trials and downfalls must *decrease*—as Our fellowship with each other must *increase.*

I want to be there with you not only during those difficult times but also during the triumphant times, as well. I desire so much to be part of your life and to share in your victories.

P.S. Seek My face, for I have already won you the victory! I promise you!

Your Father

Suggested Reading:

2 Chronicles 7:14-15; Psalm 62:1-8; Ecclesiastes 3:1-15; John 15:4

IN THE MIDST OF THE FIRE

*M*y child,

I see you struggling in certain areas of your life, areas in which I have already given you victory. If you allow those matters to become larger than they really are, they will overtake you.

Little one, remember that I have won you those victories—once and for all. However, you have to *obtain* those victories by *walking* in them. Yes, I know it is a step of faith. Even though it may seem as if you have not come out a winner, you have. You may feel as if you are losing the battle. Child, you certainly have not lost the war!

Do you think that I would allow you to be overcome in such a devastating way? Do you think that I am so cruel? I am not able! What would I benefit from it?

I am with you in the midst of the fire. I am with you through the *up*s and *down*s and every battle in which you will ever engage. When you come out of those battles victorious, in whose victory do you think that you are *sharing*, anyway? *Mine*—so how can I ever stand defeated?

Your Father

Suggested Reading:

Psalm 140; Isaiah 43:2, 12; Romans 8:26-31; 1 Corinthians 15:53-58

SEEDTIME AND HARVEST

*M*y child,

I see you struggling in the area of giving. Little one, it truly is better to give than to receive. Never once have I withheld any of My blessings from you. Is it that difficult for you to share with others?

I tell you this not to discourage you but to encourage you. When you give of yourself, unselfishly, you *allow* Me to pour out My blessings upon you.

My blessings are as continuous as the rivers of Living Water. They flow without ceasing. The more you give in My name, the more you will receive, and in full abundance.

Discipline yourself, child. If you find it so difficult to give, then give out more than what is expected of you. Not only will I bless you for it, but you will be complete in doing so.

The measure of what you give will be the measure of what you receive. Trust Me, I am always faithful—especially in the area of giving to you. My blessings await *you*.

Your Father

Suggested Reading:

Proverbs 3:27-28; Malachi 3:6-12; Luke 6:38; Acts 20:35;
2 Corinthians 8:11-12; 9:6-15

DELAYS ARE NOT DENIALS

*M*y child,

Releasing something or someone is never an easy thing to do. It truly is dying to yourself. However, when you come to the realization that it is not by your power and might but by My Spirit, you will be at rest.

Stop trying to make something work that is better left alone. A door that I close should remain closed. When I open a door you will surely know it. And when I close a door it should remain closed.

I cannot tell you enough about the consequences of forcing open a closed door or even of forcing open a door that is not quite ready to be opened. You will be in for quite a disappointment. Be patient. My perfect will for your life will not run away from you. Delays are not necessarily denials.

Little one, allow Me to finish My work. Concentrating on what you could have said differently or what you should not have said or done will only lead to more frustration—let go!

Do not be so hard on yourself, and do not limit My power. I am more than able; just be yourself! Frankly, I like it when you are just being yourself and not trying to please anyone. You are much easier to live with.

Your Father

Suggested Reading:

Hosea 2:15; Luke 11:9-10; 18:29-30; John 10:1-18; Ephesians 5:15-17

The existing of truth
does not make you free—
knowing the truth makes you free!

(See John 8:32.)

My Ways Are Not Man's

My y child,

I see your damaged and frayed feelings. My healing is flowing by My Spirit, as We speak. I promise. I *know* your pain. Little one, I felt it along with you.

Sometimes, people get beside themselves and *forget* what I have purposed them to do—to *build* and *strengthen* others, not tear down *"for the sake of the gospel or in the name of Christ."* They have chosen to use My name for their *own* purposes and agendas. I find this truly deplorable, and it demands correction. My ways are not man's, I assure you. My love is *always* unconditional. Even when the love of man runs out of patience, My love will remain faithful. I promise.

Fear not the judgment of man! Oh child, I rejoice over you with singing. I know that at times you fall short of My glory, but, little one, do not be discouraged. I will never throw it in your face. In your weakness, My strength will be made perfect in *you*. Allow Me access into those areas by releasing them to Me. I will see to your transformation.

It is that very weakness that I will use for My glory. Let Me share something with you—I am quite creative! Am I not the God of all creation? Allow Me to make something beautiful of your life. Stop allowing all this mundane criticism to burden you! Rather than being quick to receive criticism, be quick to receive My grace, and I will handle all the rest!

Your Father

Suggested Reading:

Isaiah 55:8; Jeremiah 31:1-9; Zephaniah 3:17; Colossians 2:6-23

Dear Father,

There are areas in my life that I know do not bring glory to Your name. Help me to be the child of God that You have called me to be. Cleanse me from all unrighteousness. Look not upon my sin, for I am ever falling short of Your glory.

Lord, I thank You that I am no longer held back or condemned by my unrighteousness because of the death and resurrection of Your Son, Jesus. I have been made the righteousness of God, in Christ Jesus. I am forever grateful to You, Lord.

May Your perfect will be established in my life, and may Your purpose be complete in me. Take me to that place of total surrender to Your will, so that my life may be full in You.

Prayerfully,

_____

THE BANQUETING TABLE

*M*y child,

I know you are struggling with where you belong. You are trying to fit in any way possible. Little one, you do not have to push your way through the crowds. There is plenty of room at My banqueting table for you.

Must I remind you that you are an *invited* guest? When an invitation is sent out, is it not sent out with the expectation of that person attending? I made a place there especially for you. There is a name plate that awaits you. Remember, child, there is always room for one more.

I will in no way refuse anyone at My supper table if they have been invited. If a child is hungry and asks his father for bread, would his father give him a stone? Of course not, how much *more* do you think that I will give you? My blessings are without limit!

In My family, there are no two people alike. They may appear to have similar qualities, but the truth is, the only quality they share is My love. No two people are alike. When I created you, I made you set apart from the rest—not greater but set apart. I set you apart to be unique and one of a kind—an original and not a replica.

If I wanted you to be a carbon copy of someone else, I could have easily made you so. However, it would have been a waste of life on My part. I have so much more *originality* to add to your existence. You have your own set of fears, frustrations and shortcomings. That does not disqualify you or make you in any way less or more than your brothers or sisters. Your brother or sister may appear to be perfect on the outside, but, child, they can hurt just as much as you can or even more. You are not able to see on the inside. Therefore, do not judge by appearances.

Your weakness may be their strength, and your strength may be their weakness. *Bear one another's burdens, and you that are strong are to bear the infirmities of the weak. Do this in all humility so as not to exalt yourself!*

Your Father

Suggested Reading:

Psalm 23:5-6; Matthew 7:11; 1 Corinthians 1:27-31; Philippians 2:3-5; 3:12-21

I Am the God of Promise

*M*y child,

Take heed, for I shall speak to you. Be encouraged! Do not let your heart wax cold, for I shall accomplish what I have set out to do. *All* My promises shall be *fulfilled*. Yes, My promises shall be carried out!

You will see the time come when all that I have promised shall come to pass—in *this* lifetime. I have not forgotten you, and I have not forgotten the things that I have spoken concerning your life. I have much for you, and much you shall receive!

You shall see My hand move; however, not in ways *you* have foreseen. I am not a God of mannerisms, nor will I conform to the principles of man. I am God alone! All comes to being by and through My power. There is no other way.

You have perceived My promises incorrectly. Yes, they are for you, but for Me, as well. Child, you shall witness My power, the power of My right arm. I have spoken these things to confirm My Word.

The promises that I have written for you have already come. You shall see the manifestations for yourself. You shall see signs and wonders, *confirming* the words that I have spoken to you. Therefore, do not be discouraged, for I have not forgotten you.

P.S. There is much that I have for you. Why, though, must you limit My power with time frames? I shall move!

Your Father

Suggested Reading:

Psalm 121; Isaiah 55:11; Romans 4:12b-21; 1 Peter 3:8-9

HOLD FAST TO THE VISION

*M*y child,

Never compromise your vision! For when you surrendered your will to Me, I placed *My* vision in your heart. It is *My* vision that you have adopted as your own. Do not allow the enemy to steal what I have placed within you! It is that very vision that will give you the strength to fight the good fight. The vision will *drive* you through the obstacles of resistance.

Many people will come to distract or discourage you. They may even think that you are foolish. Human reasoning will laugh in the face of those who stand in faith; however, lean not to your own understanding. My ways are not your ways. You have chosen to trust Me. How can I not honor you for that? Continue to look to Me and be encouraged, despite the criticism, child.

Remember this: That which is impossible for man, is *always* possible with Me. I am God and not man, that I should stand limited. I am *more* than able to complete what I have started. My vision shall be complete in *you*!

Your Father

Suggested Reading:

Psalm 89:19-29; Proverbs 29:18; Habakkuk 2:1-3; Romans 8:27-31; 29-36

Allow Me to Be...God

My child,

Be patient and wait upon Me! I know that you desire everything to fall into place *now*; however, the timing is not right. I am looking out for your welfare.

You are not prepared for what you are asking of Me. Little one, that does not mean I will not allow it to come to pass. My delays are not necessarily denials. I am preparing you first.

If I were to allow it to be complete now, the effect would *hinder* you more than it would benefit you, I assure you.

Your tenacity is admirable, but, child, I desire you to use that quality in other areas of your life; for instance, in the area of seeking My perfect will for your life.

Try to understand My reasoning. I am trying to spare you unnecessary pain. You have not even allowed Me the time to work out all the details. Be patient! Did you know that I rejoice in the act of blessing you? Well, I do.

Your Father

Suggested Reading:

Matthew 6:33; 7:7-8; 1 John 3:21-23; Hebrews 11:6

In the Midst of Praise

*M*y child,

I truly dwell in the midst of your praise. Did you know that I become the very thing for which you praise Me? When you praise Me for being God of *provision*, I become your *Provider*. I then supply all your needs according to *My* riches and glory. When you praise Me for being God of *healing*, I become your *Healer*.

It is so important for you to praise Me *in* all circumstances. I did not say *for* all circumstances. It is not for My benefit, but it is to benefit you. In doing so, not only will you find peace, but you allow My light to penetrate your darkness, illuminate your life and invade your present battle. I shall win it for you.

As you praise Me, you will experience true healing and deliverance. It does take *faith* to praise Me in the midst of the battle; however, it is by *faith* that you acquire the victory.

Your Father

Suggested Reading:

Psalm 42; 132:13-18; Luke 11:13; Hebrews 11:6

A Time to Give, a Time to Receive

*M*y child,

In every relationship, **effort** must be exerted on **both** sides. You cannot always expect to receive without giving, and you should not always be the giver without receiving. It takes a balance of both parties.

I know you feel as if you are giving out more than your share. Little one, in every relationship, there is bound to be conflict in this area at some point. Humble yourself! If you want the relationship to work and flourish, you are going to have to fight for it.

The devil, as small as he is, will come to sow seeds of discord among you. His main goal is to see you separated. His ultimate desire is to see you unhappy. Do not give in to his tactics!

I cannot stress enough the importance of keeping your eyes on Me. In doing so, you allow Me to bring everything else in order. Allow Me to be **fully** formed in your life, and delight yourself in My presence. Be assured, I will give you the desires of your heart.

Your Father

Suggested Reading:

Psalm 27:17; 37:1-6; Luke 6:37-42; Romans 15:1-8; 1 Peter 1:22

ONLY A GLIMPSE

*M*y child,

Sometimes, when familiar surroundings begin to disappear and you are no longer surrounded by those you know, you may feel discouraged. *I have removed the comfort that comes from mediocrity.*

You must accept the need to grow and mature. Let your faith rise within, extending outward around you! You will be amazed to see what I am able to do through those who surrender to Me *unconditionally.*

You will begin to see yourself doing things and going places that you would not ever have dreamt possible! The miracles are endless, and the blessings are limitless! Do you think that I could honestly limit those blessings? I am not able.

You have only caught a *glimpse* of what I have prepared for you. You have only begun to scratch the surface. Be assured, I am not a god of surface but God of *fullness*. My promises shall be fulfilled.

Your Father

Suggested Reading:

Romans 4:21; Ephesians 4:9-16; Philippians 3:7-16; Hebrews 6:1-3; James 1:2-6

WORDS TO LIVE BY...

God is the Author and Finisher of our faith. His Spirit *is the Holy "Ghost Writer."*

✠

ROLL WITH THE PUNCHES

*M*y child,

I know you are feeling pain. I feel it along with you. People forget My purpose and My will. My desire is to see you built up and strengthened—not torn down and left devastated. I came to give you life, not take it away!

Look to Me, child, not to man. No one knows you better than I know you. I know your strengths and your weaknesses. I will **never** remind you of your weakness nor **inhibit** you with limitations. I will, occasionally, choose to use your strengths. However, I prefer to operate in your weakness—*how I enjoy the miraculous!*

Child, never let anyone discourage you from doing what I have purposed you to do. It is not in My nature to put you down; only to put you up as hind's feet on high places.

Roll with the punches! Growth is the result of resistance and opposition. That is My reason for allowing these confrontations. I am at work.

P.S. There is no cause to worry. If everything were going smoothly, then there would be cause to be concerned. Rest in My love!

Your Father

Suggested Reading:

James 1:1-4; 2 Corinthians 12:9-10; Ephesians 4:12-16; Psalm 9

Only until you have
climbed the mountains
in your life, may you understand
the reasons for the valleys.

✝

THE ANOINTING

*M*y child,

I have called you out of darkness by name. I have called you and anointed you to fulfill My purpose. My anointing can neither be taught nor learned. It cannot be bought, sold or stolen. However, it must be protected and preserved from sinfulness.

Look not to man but to Me. Strive not to be like others! I have given you your *own* ministry—your *own* personality. In My eyes, you are special. I have personalized you for My will. I am the Author and Finisher of your faith.

There is nothing that you have to do in order to receive My anointing—just be willing to receive. You do not have to ask for My anointing: I have already given it to you. You have it. Abide in Me, and I shall abide in you.

My will shall become your will. My thoughts shall become your thoughts. My words shall become your words, and I shall direct you in every path.

Your Father

Suggested Reading:

1 Samuel 10:1; Psalm 89:19-24; Isaiah 51:16; 2 Corinthians 1:21-22; 2 Thessalonians 2:13-17; 1 John 2:24-29

HEAVENLY TREASURES

*M*y child,

How it pleases Me to see your growth. You have come a long way. As your Father, I rejoice in *your* happiness. As My child, you shall inherit everything that I have saved for you.

Though My love is unconditional, My promises *are* conditional. They require submission and obedience. Precious one, there is no other way. My love reaches all nations—Jew and Gentile, sinner and saint alike. My promises *only* reach My children. *Those who answer when I call.*

My love is pure in its fullness. It knows no boundaries nor conditions. My love cannot be contained within the depths of the sea. It, by far, transcends anything imagined by the minds of men—even yours.

P.S. Continue in My ways. You know, I find delight in your hunger for heavenly treasures. I am more than willing to bless you with them. Did you know that?

Your Father

Suggested Reading:

Nehemiah 1:5; Psalm 119:88-112; Jeremiah 32:17-19; Romans 8:7-9; Hebrews 9:15; 1 John 3:21-24

SEASONS CHANGE

*M*y child,

Seasons change and so will yours. Seasons of change are essential for growth in your life. Change requires a leap of faith. There is a time for everything. There are seasons to laugh, cry, live, die, build and tear down.

Each season has a specific *purpose* for occurring. The lessons they bring are life long, and they will lead to fulfillment within your life. Among other things, they build your *faith* and *character*. By trusting Me, you allow Me to complete what I have prepared for you.

Each season that has come and gone in your life is as solid blocks placed one by one upon each other. All are individual and separate, but come together in one solid formation.

Line upon line, precept upon precept, they have made you—*you*. Remember, little one, all things are working for the good. Yes, I know, and I love you too.

Your Father

Suggested Reading:

Ecclesiastes 3:1-8; Romans 8:28; Hebrews 11:32-40; James 1:1-4; 1 Peter 5:10-11

I Am the God of Provision

*M*y child,

Keep My ways and you shall not see or feel the plunder of defeat. Why do you fear the enemy? Little one, trust in Me. You shall not be harmed! The battle does not belong to you, but to Me. I am not man that I should stand defeated either. I go before you—stand fast, and have faith! Child, look straight and not to your right or to your left.

I am the God of *provision*. I shall provide for your every need. I desire to make *every* area of your life complete. I shall provide financially, physically and, most importantly, spiritually. I am the *Author* and *Finisher* of your faith, am I not?

I am the God of *deliverance*. As I have delivered you from the hands of the evil one, so will I deliver you from the hands of all those who *hunger* to consume your light. My light will *never* burn out.

You are as a house on top of a hill. How is it possible for you to be hidden? I have placed you before man. You are a chosen one. You shall be a vessel in which I will choose to express My glory. As you worship Me, you allow Me to be the *Healer* and *Restorer* of those who are lost and broken. Your humility has lifted you. My child, with you I am well pleased.

Your Father

Suggested Reading:

2 Samuel 2; Psalm 91; Romans 8:26-39; 2 Thessalonians 3:2-5

Bruised and Damaged

*M*y child,

I see your bruised feelings and damaged emotions. Child, I shall bring forth healing to *every* area of your life. Am I not the God of *healing* and *restoration*? Certainly, I AM!

I know you are hurting. You have been hurt by those you trusted and believed were doing My will. Child, how I desire to see you built up, and *functioning* once again.

Remember to praise Me *during* this time in your life. For I, the Lord your God, *have* delivered you from this adversity. You chose to trust Me, and I shall honor you. How can I not?

Is it not My will that you are obeying? It is. My perfect will shall be complete within you; I promise.

Your Father

Suggested Reading:

Psalm 147:2-6; Jeremiah 30:16-18; Joel 2:25-26, 32; Malachi 4:1-3; 2 Corinthians 6:3; Philippians 3:7-14

For Christ's sake,
I delight in weaknesses, in insults,
in hardships, in persecutions,
in difficulties. For when
I am weak, then I am strong.
—2 Corinthians 12:10

WORDS TO LIVE BY...

You are never the first person
to go down a rocky road.
However, you can be a first
by the way you come out.

I Require Obedience, Not Sacrifice

*M*y child,

"Religiosity" has never been one of My attributes, I assure you. Personally, I find religion to be quite inopportune and boring, to say the least.

You know that I desire *true* worship. The absence of *sincere* and *unconditional* worship results in the birth of *religion*. Were you aware of that? Child, I find it rather displeasing and quite *unacceptable*!

Never allow anyone to discourage you, because you do not conform to the ways of man. Religion was conceived by man for *man*. However, worship was created by Me for *you*. You may have not realized it before, but you do not worship Me for *My* sake—Let Me assure you of that reality. Little one, your worship allows Me to sustain *you*. By you acknowledging Me, you allow Me to acknowledge you.

How often must I remind you that your obedience to My will far outweighs anyone's meaningless sacrifice? A meaningless sacrifice is totally unacceptable. I am more interested in your submission to My will. Submitting to My will automatically leads to obeying

My commandments. Do you see, child? *Many* people obey the *written* code of the law with all its regulations; however, they neglect My will for their lives.

Those who disobey My will already break My commandments. In doing so, they are totally disregarding the law that they claim to uphold.

Where is their *true* commitment? Where there is no commitment, there is no love. Where there is no love, there is no evidence of faith. And without faith it is impossible to please me, child.

Your Father

Suggested Reading:

Isaiah 45:22-23; 29:13; Amos 5:21-24; Matthew 7:21; Mark 12:33; Romans 12:1-3; Colossians 2; Hebrews 13:15-16

THE BATTLE BELONGS TO THE LORD

*M*y child,

When dark times come, trust in Me. My light will see you through. I have come to your rescue so many times before. What makes you think now is any different?

Do you really think that I have spared you all those times of trouble to allow you to perish now, in the face of your present adversity? Come now! I am not a god of meaningless fortitude but the God of triumphant valor! I shall guard your every step.

If I go before you, be assured that no one shall come against you and prosper. I will not allow you to be defeated, for you have surrendered your will to Me. Therefore, this is My battle. The battle belongs to Me—how can I stand defeated? Oh, how it is not even a possibility! Losing has never been part of My vocabulary, neither do I want it to be part of yours. Be encouraged!

Your Father

Suggested Reading:

Genesis 28:15; Exodus 14:13-14; Deuteronomy 33:27; Psalm 37:28; Isaiah 41:10

FEATHERS IN THE WIND

*M*y child,

Occasionally, I will allow trials to happen in your life, to remind you to look to Me. Look not to man. Man will fail you, but My love will remain. All fall short of your expectancy. Man is weak, and weakness has never been known to be part of My character. Trust in Me. I am not man that I should lie or stand defeated.

Weakness of man will always surface in the midst of hurt, anger and despair. I will remind you, once again, to look unto Me. *Man will always lead you astray if your eyes do not remain on Me.*

In fits of rage or hurt, words are sometimes thrown back and forth. Words are as feathers in the wind— once released, there is no taking them back. The damage is already done. That is why you are to be quick in listening and slow in speaking.

There is power in the tongue, whether to give life or death. Little one, when someone has had a great impact on your life, it is My love, living in them, for which you have grown to care. It is My righteousness that you see within them. The strengths you see in their lives are

Mine. However, child, you cannot always live in My strength. As your Father, I must allow you to exercise **your** strength as well. This strength comes from faith in My Word.

I know the loss is difficult for you. My comfort will be with you. I have placed those people in your life to be an encouragement to you and support you during the learning and growth periods in your life. You must move on to maturity. There comes a time in your life when you must be dependent upon Me. I love you! My love truly endures forever—*unconditionally*!

Your Father

Suggested Reading:

Psalm 54; Proverbs 4:20-27; 10:12-14; Jeremiah 17:5-10

I Am Not Disappointed

My child,

Those times of your *complete* surrender to Me, I truly cherish. I have been longing to remind you of My love for you.

Those times of quietness allow My Spirit to speak to your very being, did you know that? My Words to you *sustain* your very existence. My Words give you *life*. When you seek My face, you allow Me to breathe My very life into you.

When I look upon you, child, I am not disappointed. How could I be? I have created you. Never will I be ashamed of those whom I have called by name and those who have humbled themselves before Me.

I love you with an everlasting love. Nothing shall separate you from My love, for it is that very same love that continues to give you life. It is for you and without end. I promise.

Your Father

Suggested Reading:

Isaiah 66:2; Jeremiah 31:3; Romans 8:38-39

FEELING THE FREEDOM

*M*y child,

Why is it that you have this fear of failing? Fear not! Are you not trying to please Me? Let Me inform you of a truth: It is harder to please man than it is to find favor in My eyes. Besides, what would it benefit you to please man and disobey Me in the process?

Child, do not wonder at what I am telling you. I am far more pleased when you are dependent upon Me. This fear you have of others' opinions of you is not what I desire for your life. When I created you, I did not create you to be a puppet on a string, nor do I want to see you act as one.

I have freed you from *every* bondage. Rejoice in your new found freedom. Failure? "Kingdom" ways have *never* been subject to it. Failure, along with all its shame, was forever nailed to the cross. Reach out by faith and receive the *victory* and *prosperity* that I speak into your life.

Your Father

Suggested Reading:

Isaiah 53:4-5; 1 Thessalonians 2:4; Hebrews 12:27

TREACHERY FOR TRUST

*M*y child,

I know you feel as if you have been placed within the ground floor of a pinball machine. You have been bruised and sorrowfully abused. Child, I am strengthening you. I am the One who has sustained you this far.

There are those who have tried to hold you back; however, their attempts were quite feeble, to say the least. Nevertheless, their actions were totally inappropriate and unacceptable. I know you are hurting. Little one, I feel the hurt with you. Take heart; those same brutal blows have brought you closer to Me, and for that you can be thankful.

I am *restoring* you as we speak. Child, hold no anger, bitterness or unforgiveness toward any of them. Look past the circumstance and toward the source of all their evil. That is right; you know the culprit behind the operation. Rather than taking matters into *your* own hands, allow *Me* to take care of business on both ends. Be still and know that I am God!

Your Father

Suggested Reading:

Deuteronomy 20:1; 29:29; Proverbs 2:3-5; Isaiah 43:2; Luke 12:47-48

UNCONTAINABLE BLESSINGS

*M*y child,

There is so much that I have for you. This world cannot even begin to contain the blessings that await you.

Your very existence is merely a foreshadow of what is to come. Little one, I have such dreams and hopes for your life. This world cannot begin to imagine or even understand what I have for you and am prepared to bestow upon you.

What I have prepared for you far transcends what the *natural* mind can comprehend. Why? I am limitless! Child, I know you feel limited. I will give you the strength and encouragement to go forward. Proceed, My child. I am making the crooked paths in your life *straight*. Walk in them.

Your Father

Suggested Reading:

Proverbs 3:5; Matthew 19:26; 1 Corinthians 2:9-10; Ephesians 1:9-10

But the Lord is faithful,
and he will strengthen and
protect you from the evil one.
—2 Thessalonians 3:3

VICTORY OVER DEATH

*M*y child,

Losing a friend or a loved one is never easy. It takes *time* for healing and restoration. My love and grace will be sufficient to see you through this. Allow My Spirit to comfort you.

The loss may be a separation from someone you care for, or it may be as devastating as a death of someone close to you. Child, I feel your pain. I love you so much that I sent My only Son for you. He died for man by the hands of man. Oh, how I feel your pain! I am not unsympathetic to your pain.

However, little one, death is forever swallowed up in victory! You have the victory through My Son. Just as you have been "crucified" with Him, it is no longer you who lives, but He who lives in you. Sharing His death has allowed you to share in His resurrection. You shall begin anew, and, yes, you shall experience joy again. You shall even laugh again. My joy shall flow without end.

Look to Me for comfort, and My Spirit shall descend upon you as a dove and give you the peace you thought was impossible. I shall see you through this; I promise.

Your Father

Suggested Reading:

Psalm 30:5; Ecclesiastes 8:6-8; Isaiah 51:3; 66:13; John 16:33

SPRINGS OF LIFE

*M*y child,

I will speak to you. As in times before, I have told you to seek My face. Then, and *only* then, will you experience and know perfect peace. You have asked, "How can I love You more, Lord?" I have answered you, *"Seek My face, and obey My voice."*

Those who obey Me, fear Me—for the friendship with God is with those who fear Him. The fear of the Lord is the beginning of wisdom, and, through that fear, I have imparted such wisdom unto you.

Wisdom has flowed from Me and poured out into your life, filling every void.

I am doing what I had promised unto you at an *earlier* time in your life. Seasons have come and gone, yet your faithfulness unto Me remains. As good fruit is picked from a tree, leaving what is unprofitable, so I have picked what is good and removed what I would not have remain.

My beloved, I am strengthening you even now. It is so important and necessary that I remind you of this reality, for you shall not see defeat! How could I have it any other way? Little one, I love you, and you know this to be true. How can I withhold any good thing from you? I am certainly not able! I shall provide a way for you in the desert. I shall cause wells to spring up within you and cause you to be carried away by waves of *Living Water.* I shall lead you into springs of life and into waters that will leave you fulfilled and renewed.

Child, you have watched and prayed, and I have heard. I will come to your rescue. And I assure you this day that I shall be the God of *deliverance* for you.

Your Father

Suggested Reading:

Psalm 84:5-6; 103:17-18; 114:7-8; Proverbs 11:30; Isaiah 43:19; 58:9-14; John 7:37-38

VALLEY OF DECISION

*M*y child,

I know that you are faced with making an important decision. It will affect the rest of your life. I know you feel overwhelmed and confused, and oppression is beginning to settle. Little one, confusion is not of Me, and I would never **overwhelm** you with a decision that I thought you were unable to make. Right now, you are so afraid of making the wrong decision, it has left you undecided. Child, lack of faith is not My will for your life.

Indecision is not of Me nor is it part of My vocabulary. If you are unable to make a decision because of the fear of failing, you are not exercising faith. It displeases Me to see you not having faith. It is not for **My** benefit that you exercise faith; it is for **you**. Having faith to trust Me allows Me to accomplish what is best for your life.

My child, when **you** asked for this opportunity long ago, you did not question My will and ability then, right? Then why do you question Me now? I am more than able to fulfill what I have promised. By faith you asked for it, so by faith you must **receive**. The decision to receive it or not is all yours.

Your Father

Suggested Reading:

Mark 11:22-25; Romans 1:17; 4:21; Hebrews 11:1, 6; 2 Corinthians 1:20; James 2:14-18, 26

Here I am! I stand at the door and
knock. If anyone hears my voice and
opens the door, I will come in and eat
with him, and he with me.

—Revelation 3:20

Desire, Discipline—Delight

*M*y child,

I am not self-centered when I ask you to praise Me; I am not able. Do you honestly believe that I would be that selfish? When I created you, I gave you a free will to choose. Little one, the choice always belongs to you; therefore, *choose* life.

Choice can be such a beautiful concept. I will never force you to do anything you do not want to do—how could I find pleasure in such an act? However, I do want you to be *submissive* to My will. Therein lies the blessing.

When you choose to express your love for Me out of your *own* free will, not expecting anything in return, it blesses Me. Do you think it pleases Me to know that someone would only praise Me when I offer something in return? Praise can only come from a heart of *thanksgiving.*

Child, I am *always* willing to bless you. I know your desires before you even ask—; Nevertheless, seek My face as well as My hand. I am a jealous and holy God. I desire that nothing separates you from My love, and nothing shall! Seek first My kingdom; then everything else will merely be "added" to you.

Your Father

Suggested Reading:

1 Chronicles 16:27-34; Psalm 8; 95:6; John 4:24

The "Gift-Giver"

*M*y child,

I have brought you many gifts. Child, they have been given to you so that you would *share* with others. A gift is not a gift unless it is *given*. You are My child; however, you are one of *many* children. These gifts have been imparted into your life. They are not a result of what you have or have not done. It is by My grace that you have been given them.

Be led by Me, and Me alone! Show My love to *everyone* that is willing to hear, for that is the task that I have prepared for you. Have no fear and trust Me, for I am at your side with joy and hope that will keep you. I am your Savior, and I am for all who believe in Me.

Your Father

Suggested Reading:

Romans 11:29; 12:3-8; 1 Corinthians 12:12-31; 2 Timothy 1:6-10; 1 Peter 4:7-11

Dear Father,

How I desire a pure heart, the heart of a *true* servant. Lord, search my heart. I ask that You would remove any unforgiveness, bitterness or resentment that is hidden in me. Replace them with love, mercy and compassion.

As You have shown me grace, help me to do the same for others. Father, I pray for a deeper revelation of Your pure love. Then, and only then, may I begin to understand and even share that love with others.

I know it must begin with me. Help me to forgive myself and accept myself the way You made me. I will then be able to accept others the way You made them.

Sincerely,

_____

IN PREPARATION

*M*y child,

Be at peace, for I am preparing the way for you at this very moment. How it pleases Me to see your exuberance when it comes to the heavenly vision. You know, the very *vision* within you is *My* vision. I have created you for My purpose. I have placed My thoughts within you. I have replaced your will with My own and placed My words within your mouth. I have done this at your request. How My heart leaps for joy!

My beloved, the time has come for you to go forth and spread My Word. The time of healing and restoration has taken its course. The seasons have come and gone and have completed their purpose. I have built you up—have you not noticed? I have brought healing to your very existence. How I love to bring forth My healing and restoring power upon *you.*

I rejoice when you are rejoicing, and I weep along with you as your tears are shed. My little one, I have seen your pain, and I have collected each one of those tears. Not even one of those precious tears has slipped through My hands. Yes, I have seen your tears. I have held you close in My arms as they have washed My feet. Beloved, rejoice! I have made you whole.

Your Father

Suggested Reading:

Psalm 34:17-19; 126

Do Not Fear–Take Courage

*M*y child,

There are so many areas of your life that I have yet to bring to full maturity. In sudden fits of anger, your old nature has come to the surface. Have you noticed? Do not fear nor be discouraged, I will remind you that you are a new creation. You shall not lack in any way!

The old has surfaced for one purpose: It is to remind you of *My* righteousness—for all fall short of My glory, and so do *you*. I have made room for your mistakes; let Me comfort you in that. At times, you will witness the weakness of man by *your* reaction to the circumstances that surround you.

However, I do not want you to be swept away in a current of emotion. It is natural to have feelings, but they should not *always* dictate how you are to behave. I desire faith to be the motivation behind your actions and love to be the root. Remain in My love, and receive My grace—the same grace available to all who receive My love.

Your Father

Suggested Reading:

Romans 8:1-17; 1 Corinthians 9:19-27; 2 Corinthians 12:1-10

IN THE FULLNESS OF TIME

My child,

Your prayers never go unanswered by Me. I know you feel as if I do not hear you, but I do. Little one, sometimes you ask Me for the very last thing you need. Trust Me, I truly am at work. Do not be anxious for the things that will surely come. Yes, they *will* come. However, they will come in the fullness of time—*My* time.

Have faith and *expect* these things; however, do not be overwhelmed by them not occurring just now. You *must* learn to be patient.

I have begun a good work, and I am more than able to finish what I have started. Continue in My ways and look to Me. Seek first My kingdom and not yours. Seek My righteousness, and I shall give you the very desires of your heart; I promise.

Your Father

Suggested Reading:

Psalm 34:17; Isaiah 65:24; Jeremiah 17:5-10; 33:2-3

The Blessings Are Flowing

*M*y child,

How many times do I have to tell you to trust Me? I am at work. I can assure you of that. Who do you think has brought you this far? It has not been by *your* own strength?

These victories that you are now experiencing are merely the beginning of the new life with which I have blessed you. Enjoy, My child; I have given you the *victory*! There is no need to fear nor expect defeat in any way. Trust Me, child, *the blessings are flowing*; I promise!

Your Father

Suggested Reading:

Deuteronomy 28:1-14; Psalm 25:1-5; 60:12; Zechariah 4:6-7; 2 Corinthians 5:17

THE RECOVERY ROOM

*M*y child,

I know going back can sometimes be a difficult task, and *only* My grace can get you through the experience. Do you now see how much your heart and mind will *hide* past hurts without you even realizing it?

There are rooms that you would rather not enter. There are doors that you would rather have remain closed. However, child, I cannot allow this to continue.

When you gave your life to Me, you gave Me *everything*. Slowly, I began to work in you. I removed those areas in your life that would not glorify Me. Your began to break bad habits—your speech changed, your attitudes began to soften one at a time and your selfish motives began to become non-existent. Haven't you noticed?

Do you now see how far I have brought you? I am the *Author* and *Perfector* of your faith. As you slowly began to submit to My perfect will, I began to mold you into a vessel I can use. However, there are certain areas of your life that you have not yet surrendered to Me.

You have allowed unforgiveness, past hurts and bitterness to take root. They have become such a part of your life, you do not even realize their presence. This ought not to be. Some, you have simply grown used to, and others you would rather not face. Consequently, I am doing a new thing in your life! Sometimes, going back is necessary to go forward. That is the reason for all these matters to be surfacing now. I am bringing you to another level—*unspeakable joy*!!

In order for this transformation to take place, you must *release* everything—including the *scars*. Leave the healing process to Me, for My healing and restoration power is at work. You will be pleased with the end result. I promise!

Your Father

Suggested Reading:

Isaiah 64:8; Jeremiah 17:14; 31:1-5; Ezekiel 36:22-32; 2 Corinthians 5:17

SEASON OF SECLUSION

My child,

I have brought you from being dependent upon others to a place of trusting *Me*. Child, others will give *their* own opinions and views; however, My desire is for you to seek *Me* for the answers to your questions. No one knows you better than I do.

I know you are easily overwhelmed with thoughts of failure, but child, trust Me. I have never left your side, neither do I intend to do so. I am bringing you to a level of *greater* commitment—a season of "seclusion." I am requiring leaps of faith on your part, to seek My face *during* your adversities. I am also requiring statements of faith. Give Me the glory as the Provider in your life.

I know you feel as if you are all alone, and everyone has left your side. Child, remember My Son, Jesus. His friends *slept* as He *wept* for His life. Never will I leave you or forsake you. Even when you turn away, I remain faithful to you until the very end.

Man will *inevitably* fall short of My glory and *continually* fall short of your expectancy. However, with Me, expect plenty and receive *much*!

Your Father

Suggested Reading:

Mark 6:31; 14:32-42; Luke 22:39-46

AS IN TIMES BEFORE

My child,

I have laid up many riches for you, riches that are yet to be revealed. These many riches are uncontainable. *Continue* to seek My face! Hear Me, child; I have much for you! It is much that you shall receive! You have humbled yourself in My presence—I shall lift you up.

Beloved, with you I am well pleased. You have sought Me, and how is it possible for Me to deny Myself to you? I am not able. I shall give you the desires of your heart. My desires are fulfilled in you. My joy is complete in you. My child, My joy is full in you.

My love is flowing upon you this very hour, for you have sought the Lord your God in the midnight hour. You have hearkened unto Me, and I have hearkened unto you. I love you with an everlasting love. My peace is upon you. Therefore, stand and hold fast to My Word. I have spoken to you, and you know this to be true.

This is not of your own understanding. As in times before, I have told you to lean not to your own understanding, for My ways are not yours. Child, continue in My will. I have placed an open door before you. Be humble, yet be bold and walk through it. The door that I have opened for you is a door through which you must go. It is not for Me but for *you* to go through.

Trust in Me—I shall never lead you astray! It is not in My nature to lead you anywhere I have not been Myself. Be bold and be strong, for I shall be with you—and you know the Lord your God has spoken.

I shall provide a way where there is no way. I am the God of possibilities. I make impossibilities into *possibilities*. Watch and see Me work!

Your Father

Suggested Reading:

Genesis 28:15; Psalm 119:133; Isaiah 42:16; 43:1-2; Matthew 6:19-21; Ephesians 1:18

Love never looks
to see what time it is
when a friend calls for help.

WORDS TO LIVE BY...

More strength is obtained
from loving your worst enemy
than agreeing
with your best friend.

COME BACK TO ME

*M*y child,

Come back to Me. Oh, how My heart aches for the sound of your voice. How I have longed for *you*. Little one, it is not I who has done this to you. I am not able! *Blessings* and *goodness* are Mine. I desire to share them with you. I have not come into your life to bring torment. It is not even a possibility! I give you peace.

My beloved, *return* to Me. I have desired your face to be near Mine. Turn not your heart from Me. *How I love you with an everlasting love!* I am unable to contain it. I would not even attempt to do so. I give you joy and peace. Your *present* struggle is not of My hands; I assure you. I have come to give you life.

Turn not your eyes from Me. Allow Me to be the Light in your *present* darkness. Trust Me and follow My voice. I shall not lead you astray or cause your foot to slip. You are My child, and I love you eternally. Seek Me again! I miss your presence before Me. Yes, I miss *your* presence. Little one, trust Me. This shall surely pass, but My truth and love for you shall live forever. Nothing shall separate you from My love.

My heart cries out for you! Can you not hear? Do you not know? I have given My life for you. Look at the scars upon My hands—they speak of sacrifice. My love for you is so great, but you have not understood. I came to give life, not take it. I have seen you searching. Look to Me—I AM what you seek.

Your Father

Suggested Reading:

Deuteronomy 30; Lamentations 3:22-23; 5:4; Joel 2:11-14; John 10:7-16; Acts 3:19

Open During Construction

*M*y child,

I know you feel as if you are being *stretched* to the limits, but be strong. I am building a *new* foundation in your life. In order for me to do so, some of the *old* walls need to come down. The structure is shaky and unstable. I am making all things new; however, in order to do this, I am doing away with the old and blessing you with the new.

I will tell you again. You have allowed past hurts, bitterness and resentment to take root. They have begun to affect the durability of your foundation. Bitterness will eat away at the walls and leave your heart in ruins.

I am beginning to heal those places deep within your heart; however, you must allow Me to work in those areas that you have shut away from everyone else. Allow Me access, child. I will *never* use those hurts to hurt you; I promise.

I am also clearing away the rubble...this very moment. When you surrender your heart to Me, you must allow Me access to *all* areas. These areas *include* the *unreachable* wastelands.

Little one, you have allowed those hurts to become such a part of your life that you have accepted them as normal. Do not allow those bad experiences to give you a negative and distorted outlook on life. Your life is too precious to hold on to offenses and be burdened by them. Be loosed and let go! Allow forgiveness to flow and healing to begin.

My plans for you far exceed what your mind can imagine or even comprehend. In order for all that I have purposed to come to pass, healing *must* take place. *Healing* and *restoration* are the *beginning* of a firm foundation. Allow *Me* to do the constructing. Once again, I am building a new foundation—one that will endure the seasons that have yet to pass.

In a way, I am building a "new" you. And trust Me, you will be pleased with the end result. I know that I am.

Your Father

Suggested Reading:

Isaiah 43:18-19; 58:11; Jeremiah 17:14; 30:17; Ezekiel 36:26-27, 33-38; Hebrews 12:15

TEMPTATION WILL COME

*M*y child,

As long as there remains life in your body, you will be tempted. Temptation will always come; it is not sinful to be tempted. The sin is committed when one *yields* to the temptation. You have been given victory over every temptation. Even Jesus was tempted, but He was found without sin. However, child, *you* will fall short. Know that for every temptation, I have given you a way out.

I do not tempt anyone. When I give to My children, I bless—blessings that lead to life and life in abundance. How could I do it any other way? I am not able. I see your frustration and anger. You have said no and yet have yielded to temptation. You have fallen, but you must get back up once again.

You must come to a decision. Do you want this sin to be part of your life or not? When you submit your life, totally, to Me, resist the devil's temptation. Come against him with My Word. Do not *allow* him a hold in your life. If you give him an inch, he will take a yard. However, until you decide for yourself, he will continue to use your greatest weakness against you.

Once you make the decision—as hard as it may be—by the power of My Word, he must leave you! All this is a result of submitting to My Word and being obedient to My will. My Word is truth, and that truth will make you free. Also, remember the peace and forgiveness that follows true repentance.

Your Father

Suggested Reading:

John 8:31b-32; 1 Corinthians 10:13; 2 Corinthians 1:10; James 1:12; 4:7; 1 Peter 5:8-11

TRIALS AND TRIBULATIONS

*M*y child,

It is My desire to see you strengthened and encouraged. It is not in My nature to do otherwise. I am building a *new* foundation. I am restoring brokenness and am breaking down barriers in your life.

Part of the turmoil that you are in now is just the pain felt before your deliverance. As a mother feels the birth pangs before the delivery of her baby, so are you experiencing the pangs before the delivery of the new you. I promise you new life!

I am the God of deliverance. I am delivering you from your *present* trial. However, I am allowing certain matters that would normally have been secret to be revealed. I have done this in order for you to see them. This is not to overwhelm you or discourage you, but for you to overcome and learn from the experience.

I know you do not understand why these incidents are occurring. Child, give those "whys" and "how comes" to Me. I have My reasons. My purpose will always prevail above man's plans. Trust Me, you have chosen to do My will. How can I not honor your submission to Me? You have chosen to hear My voice rather than settling for the voice of criticism and the opinions of man.

Oh, how much opposition will come your way. However, hold fast! Cling to My Word, for My Word is truth, and that truth will make you free; I promise!

Your Father

Suggested Reading:

Psalm 26:1-12; 32:7-11; 33:4-22; Proverbs 16:9; 19:21; 1 Peter 1:3-7; 2 Corinthians 4:16-18

THE ELEVENTH HOUR

*M*y child,

I shall dwell with you. I shall make this My abode. This house shall become My sanctuary, for I have been welcomed into this place. This shall be My dwelling place.

I shall not dwell with man much longer. The time is drawing near for Jesus to return for His bride—the church. I am here to prepare her, to strengthen her, to build her and to bring forth healing. Yes, I have come to heal her. I have seen her brokenness; I have seen her pain. And, yes, I have seen her disobedience.

I am coming soon, says the Lord God. I shall come in all My glory and splendor. Prepare yourself, says the Lord. Prepare yourself for the coming of the Lord. I am making straight the way. I am coming soon! Look around, can you not see? Can you not hear? Fear not, but take heart, My child.

The final hour has come for the bride to make herself ready for her Bridegroom. He shall come in glory and splendor. He shall return for a church without spot or wrinkle. Therefore, prepare yourself, My child. This is the hour to believe My Word. For the hour of destruction and desolation is upon you. Do not fear, for I am *near* you, and I am *with* you. You will be with Me. You will look upon Me, and I will look upon you in all your beauty.

Your Father

Suggested Reading:

Matthew 24-25; Revelation 3:20-21; 16:15

WHO'S CALLING THE SHOTS?

My child,

Quit complaining! Your grumbling shall *delay* My promises even further. Let Me remind you, I am under no obligation to serve *you*. I am under obligation to perform My Word. When I made a promise to you, I had no reservations. Therefore, have none about Me or My ability.

May I see some faith on your part? Part of receiving the promise is receiving without seeing. Your maturity, or lack thereof, has hindered you. It has kept you from the promise. Humble yourself before Me, or I shall do it for you. I am not *your* Servant, nor do I intend to be. You must open your heart to Me for the purpose of *change*.

You have not received, because you have asked incorrectly. You have asked for the dessert prior to eating the main course. I have made preparations for the meal, and you have disregarded the meal for the *nobility* of the dessert. Oh, there is much need for growth.

Dig deep into My Word for the meat! You have been tenderized long enough in the milk. Be no longer a mere *hearer* of the Word—*DO*. I require action. We shall discuss this again; I promise.

Your Father

Suggested Reading:

Hebrews 5:12-14; 6:9-20; James 1:22-23

✝

Dear Father,

This is such a difficult time in my life. Lord, I really need Your strength and encouragement now. I do not understand why certain things are happening, but I will trust You.

You have never failed me, Lord. I know You would never do so. You have brought me through struggles so many times before. Why should now be any different?

I know if I trust You, You will give me grace through it all. I will be able to look back on this period of my life and see Your hand guiding and even carrying me every step of the way.

Trustingly,

_____

WHOOP GLORY!

My child,

Line upon line and precept upon precept, I am building you. I am building character in you. Yes, strong character that will last and will not sway or falter—integrity.

Hold fast to My Word, for I *will* accomplish what I said I would do. Take courage; this day shall prove its worth. I shall cause blessing to break forth. My glory shall break forth as the noonday. You shall see My glory made manifest in your life.

As the dawn breaks, so have *you* been broken to give room for the newness of a brand-new day. Rejoice! All things are new. I shall show you the power of My wonder. Take courage, for I shall watch over you. I will watch over My Word to perform it. I promise.

Rejoice, *your* time has come. You have waited and sought My will; therefore, I shall reward you. Blessings, blessings and *more* blessings are for you to receive. You have not trusted in vain; you have not believed in vain, and you have not sown in vain. I will show you My faithfulness; I will show you My abundance, and I will show you My hand. Praise Me!

Your Father

Suggested Reading:

Deuteronomy 30; Psalm 8; 19; Proverbs 3:1-26

Blessings Require Obedience

My y child,

Obedience and submission are what I require of you. You are in a day and age where sin and rebellion have become a way of life. However, it shall not become a way for you; continue in My Word. My Word shall bring conviction. It shall bring reproof and correction. My Word shall lead you into a life of righteousness.

Be holy, for I am holy. I desire to bring My church back into holiness. I desire to bring *you* back into holiness.

Enough of trying to do things *your* way; it is time to return to *My* way—the *only* true way. My way gives life. My way ensures life. Search My Word, and you shall see the truth. My Word revealed to you shall bring you to a level of obedience that leads to prosperity. Yes, prosperity—prosperity shall no longer be a negative word in My church. Too long, the term "prosperity" has been used and abused by those who are *far* from Me, causing others to push My hand of blessing away. However, I have called you close to My heart, and I am calling you to a level of prosperity—not poverty.

I AM the God of prosperity, and, not only shall I bring financial stability back to My church, but I will bring stability in *every* area. Never put a temporal meaning on something that is eternal. My promises are fulfilled, and My blessings are without limit. Rejoice! They are for *you*!

Your Father

Suggested Reading:

Deuteronomy 28; Psalm 37:3-7, 17-34; Proverbs 3; 2 Timothy 3:16

WAKE, O SLEEPER

*M*y child,

I shall bring revival to My church. It shall begin with you. I will revive you and bring you back to a place of *burning* desire for My Word, My presence and My will. Die to yourself, and rid yourself of *all* selfishness. I am not able to work in, on behalf of or through children of disobedience. I require CHANGE.

I shall bring *change*. However, change comes at a price—repentance and reformation. You must cast off the bondage of sin and tradition. You must rid yourself of all that separates us. I shall bring illumination and revelation.

What has been, I have allowed. However, I shall tolerate it no longer. You cannot remain the same. Wake from your slumber, and come alive to the voice of My Spirit. Take heed to My correction, for My correction brings life, but your continual disobedience shall bring death.

Continue no longer in your former ways! What does light have to do with darkness? Absolutely, nothing. I have brought you revelation and given you knowledge; however, you have stumbled in disobedience. Knowledge brings responsibility. Yes, you are responsible to walk uprightly, uncompromisingly and *fruitfully* in that knowledge.

CHANGE I *require,* and CHANGE I shall see. Rejoice in My chastisement, for I have displayed My love for you this day.

Your Father

Suggested Reading:

Ezekiel 18:27-32; 20:33-35; 37:1-14; Acts 2:16-21

MOVING ON TO MATURITY

*M*y child,

Release your cares to Me; I am doing a new thing in the earth. Leave your hurts behind you, and leave room for My healing. You limit what I am able to do for you when you hold on to pain and unforgiveness. Allow Me to bring forth healing.

Stop your judgment! You bring judgment upon yourself when you blame others for some of *your* mistakes. You must learn in order to grow and mature. How can you grow when you have held on to your past? How can you move on when you have chosen not to forgive?

Repent! Your pride has kept you from receiving My forgiveness. Your pride has held you back from receiving My blessings, the blessings that I have intended for *you*. Pride shall cause you to fall.

I tell you this day to change your ways! I am coming soon; purge yourself of all wickedness, of all malice and of all unrighteousness. The measure that you show unforgiveness is the measure you shall receive it in return. Any questions?

Your Father

Suggested Reading:

Proverbs 16:18; Matthew 7:1-6; 6:14-15; Luke 6:35-38

Welcome to the "100-Fold"

*M*y child,

The time has come. As I have told you in times past, I have prepared a place for you. I know that you have waited. And, child, your perseverance shall reward you. Be encouraged this day. You shall see every one of My blessings *fulfilled*.

I have called you. I named you *before* the time of your conception. I created you with *My* own hand. How I love you with an everlasting love.

I have such wonderful plans for your life. These are not mere words, for I am not a god of mere words. I am the God of power. You shall experience that power, not because others have told you but because I have told you.

You shall see My glory and power for *yourself*. You shall not be a *spectator* but a *participator*. Rejoice, for your God does. I rejoice in you, child. I love you, and I have prepared you—welcome!

Your Father

Suggested Reading:

Psalm 119:49-50; Isaiah 43:18-21; Jeremiah 31:2-4; John 4:42

TIME WILL TELL

*M*y child,

Take heed, for I shall speak to you. Be encouraged! Do not let your heart wax cold, for I shall accomplish what I have set out to do. My promises shall be fulfilled. Yes! My promises shall be carried out. You will see the time come; you will see all that I have promised come to pass.

I have not forgotten you, and I have not forgotten the things that I have spoken concerning your life. I have much for you. The time is now to see My hand move. You shall see My hand move but not in ways *you* have foreseen. I am not a god of *mannerisms*, nor will I conform to the principles of man.

I am God—alone. All comes into being by and through *My* power. There is no other way. You have perceived My promises incorrectly. Yes, they are for you, but they are for Me as well. You shall witness My power—the power of My right arm. I have spoken these things to confirm My Word.

The promises that I have written for you have already come. You shall see the *manifestations* for yourself. You shall see signs and wonders confirming the Word that I have spoken to you. Do not be discouraged, for I have not forgotten you. Remember **Me.** Why must you limit My power with time frames? I will move; seek My face continually.

Your Father

Suggested Reading:

Psalm 37:3-7; Proverbs 3:5-6; Romans 4:14-22; 1 Peter 5:7

TIMES OF PRUNING

*M*y child,

Learn to enter My rest. You must understand the meaning of this word. I have finished the work. There is nothing you need to add to what I have already done. In times that you should have been at rest, you have labored. In times that you should have been laboring, you have rested. This ought not to be. However, be encouraged, for I am at work in you.

I assure you, I am rebuilding what the enemy has torn down. Some things have been torn down at My request. I will not allow unfruitfulness to be a part of your life. I will cause *new* fruit to be seen in you—long lasting fruit. You will know that I, by My Spirit, have birthed this fruit in you. Rejoice, for your time of preparation is short. I shall cause your righteousness to shine forth. Rejoice! I do, and so should you!

Your Father

Suggested Reading:

Joshua 1:13; Matthew 11:28-30; Romans 3:21-28; Galatians 3:11; Hebrews 4

The Hour of Grace

*M*y child,

Take note of what I tell you this day: you shall see the wonder of My power, and you shall see My hand work for *you*. Therefore, be encouraged, for I shall move on your behalf. I shall cause rivers to give life to *all* the desert places. Be filled, and I will cause victory to break forth on your left and on your right.

I call you My beloved, for I truly love you. Receive the love that I have for you. Keep the faith; I will surely move! *This is the hour of My grace to work for you* on behalf of the *vision—My* vision.

I have only just begun. You shall be blessed, very blessed. I am God and not man that I should lie. I shall deliver you and use you. Yes, your redemption draws near—*very* near.

Your Father

Suggested Reading:

Psalm 1:1-3; Isaiah 12; John 4:7-24; 7:37-39

CALL TO THE HARVEST

"For you know the grace of our Lord Jesus Christ, that though He was rich, yet for your sakes He became poor, so that through His poverty you might become rich" (2 Cor. 8:9, NKJV). Jesus, Himself, told His disciples that there was always going to be poverty in this world. He came to save the lost, heal the sick and feed the hungry. He did not only feed them food, He fed them life. He fed them with the Word of God. He quoted Scripture, *"...man shall not live by bread alone, but by every word that proceeds from the mouth of God"* (Matt. 4:4, NKJV).

As food is a necessity for the body, the Word of God is essential for the spirit man to live. In those quiet times before Him, the Word that He speaks to our beings becomes the very breath of life. This is the *only* way our existence can be sustained. His grace and mercy being poured into our lives renews us daily. He gives us the encouragement and faith to press on toward the calling that He has prepared for us.

Jesus came to the poor, sick, outcast and socially unaccepted. Even though they were at the lowest point of their lives; even when they felt all hope was gone, or even if they did not think there was a chance, He made a way! They had tried everything else. There was no other hope outside of their despair. Nevertheless, Jesus met them at their lowest point.

The rich did not accept Him. Why? He taught that it was the condition of the heart that was important and not financial status. This angered the religious. They were interested in keeping their outward fronts in an attempt to hide their inward corruption. However, Jesus saw right through their hypocrisy—to their hearts.

It is not money, material possessions, or any good works that you may do that will guarantee you your salvation. Jesus is the only way to the Father—the only true God. Jesus is the *WAY*, the *TRUTH*, and the *LIFE*. We all know there have been times when we have needed our friends or to be loved by our parents. There have been times we have not been appreciated by our wife or husband, we felt we did not belong, or we were used and abused by someone we trusted. Perhaps there was a time when the drugs or alcohol wore off, and the problem was still there—bigger than ever. Or maybe everything in your life is going well, but there *still* is an emptiness that you cannot exactly pinpoint. You have questions about life: *Is this what life's all about? Why do I feel so empty inside? What is my purpose in life? Why do I feel that I have nothing to offer? Why am I always struggling with myself?*

We will all fail each other at one time or another. However, there is Someone there. He has always been there to offer us help, hope and answers to these questions. However, we have been so clouded by our circumstances or dulled by our sinfulness, that we have not been able to hear. He is a friend that sticks closer than a brother or sister. He loves us—He loves *you*! The Bible says, *"...greater love has no man than this, than to lay down one's life for his friends" (John 15:13, NKJV).* Jesus died for us; He died for *you*. It was through His death that we may experience life.

My friend, I ask you a very important question. Before you answer this question, I ask you to really think about your answer first. If you were to pass from this life, at this very moment, do you know where you would spend eternity? Would you spend eternity in heaven with God and His Son, Jesus? Or would you spend eternity in a place where this world in all its evil and corruption is merely a glimpse of what will be in store for some? This place is hell, and it is real!

If you answered the first question, "heaven," then ask yourself this question: *Am I born again?* What does it mean to be born again? It means a spiritual rebirth or turning from your evil ways. *"If My people, who are called by My name will humble themselves, and pray and seek My face, and turn from their wicked ways, then will I hear from heaven, and will forgive their sin..." (2 Chron. 7:14, NKJV).*

You may even think that you are not really a bad person who has "evil ways," *"there is no one righteous, not even one" (Rom. 3:10, NKJV). "...for all have sinned and fall short of the glory of God" (Rom. 3:23). "For it is by grace you have been saved, through faith—and this not from yourselves, it is the gift of God—not by works, so that no one boast" (Eph. 2:8-9).*

What does it mean—we are saved by grace? First, grace means undeserved favor or unwarranted love that God shows us through His salvation. It is not by good works that we receive salvation—it is a gift.

How does sin affect you, and what is the penalty? Sin separates you from the presence of God. This separation from God is spiritual death and will lead to eternal damnation. *"For the wages of sin is death, but the gift of God is eternal life in Christ Jesus our Lord" (Rom. 6:23). "Therefore, just as sin entered the world through one man, and death through sin, and in this way death came to all men, because all sinned" (Rom. 5:12).*

However, God did give us a *second* chance in life. If you ask Jesus Christ to come into your heart and take residence in your life, and if you confess with your mouth that He is Lord, your sins will be forgiven, and you shall be saved! *"For God so loved the world that He gave His only begotten Son, that whoever believes in Him should not perish but have everlasting life" (John 3:16, NKJV).*

Only you can make the decision to accept Him or not. It is by your own free will. He will never force you to make this very important decision; however, He will warn you of the consequences of avoiding it. Jesus paid a price for your salvation through His life. You have to pay a price, too; you must give Him your life. Be dead to sin and alive to Christ. *"What shall we say, then? Shall we go on sinning so that grace may increase? By no means! We died to sin; how can we live in it any longer?" (Rom. 6:1-2).*

Jesus said, *"If anyone would come after me, he must deny himself and take up his cross and follow me. For whoever wants to save his life will lose it, but whoever loses his life for me will find it" (Matt. 16:24-25).*

If you want to make the decision to accept Jesus Christ as your personal Savior and Lord, please pray the following prayer. It will be the most important decision that you will ever make. However, please make it while the decision is still *yours* to make...

God, I know that I am a sinner, and I believe You sent Your Son, Jesus, who died on the cross for my sins. The blood that He shed on the cross washes me clean. I go now in the victory of the cross and resurrection. Jesus, I accept You into my life. Give me the power to overcome every temptation of the devil. I renounce his works and deny him any further access into my life. Holy Spirit of God, there are things I still do not understand, but I pray that You will fill in the missing pieces. Jesus, I will look to You as the Author and Perfector of my faith.

If you have chosen to accept Jesus today and prayed this prayer, *welcome to the family of God!* We would love to hear from you. Maybe you have a prayer request and need agreement in prayer. If you would like to receive the monthly newsletter titled, *Abundant Life*, please write to the address below. May the Lord Jesus Christ bless you!

Michael J. Lusardi
Salvation House
P.O. Box 83243
San Diego, CA 92138-3243
Website: www.hearhisvoice.com
Email: michael@hearhisvoice.com

GOD'S WORD CONCERNING...

Doubt and fear..........Isaiah 41:10; Romans 4:21; Ephesians 3:12; Psalm 4:3; 84:11; 112:7

Finances.................... Malachi 3:8–12; Philippians 4:19; Luke 11:9; 12:24, 30; Matthew 7:11; Mark 11:24

Friends......................1 Corinthians 15:33; 1 John 1:7; 2 Corinthians 6:17; Proverbs 2:20; 13:20; 18:24

Grief..........................Psalm 23:4; 34:18; 51:17; 147:3; Isaiah 61:1–3; 2 Thessalonians 2:16, 17

Guidance...................Psalm 32:8; 37; 73:24; Proverbs 3:6; John 16:13; Luke 1:79

Guilt.......................... Romans 8:1, 30; 1 John 1:9; Acts 13:39; Isaiah 53:5; Matthew 12:31, 32

Happiness................. Nehemiah 8:10; Psalm 40:3; 64:10; Proverbs 16:20; 1 Peter 1:8

Inadequacy................ 1 Corinthians 1:30; Psalm 1:3; Hebrews 4:16; Ephesians 2:1, 6; Isaiah 45:24; Galatians 2:20; Romans 9:37

Loneliness.................Hebrews 13:5; 1 John 1:3; Jeremiah 31:3; Proverbs 18:24; Revelation 3:20; Psalms 37:28

Patience.................... Hebrews 10:36; Galatians 6:9; Ecclesiastes 3:1; James 1:3, 4, 12; Psalm 27:14; Romans 15:5; Isaiah 40:31

Peace of Mind.......... Psalm 23; 29; 85; Isaiah 32:17;
2 Timothy 1:7

Persecution.............. Matthew 5:10, 44, 45;
1 Peter 4:12–14; Luke 6:37; Psalm 103:6

Prayerlessness............ Isaiah 43:22; Zephaniah 1:6;
Daniel 9:13; Luke 2:37; 6:12; 1 Thessalonians 3:10

Protection................. Genesis 28:15; Psalm 18:32;
27:1; 34:7, 19; Proverbs 18:10

Salvation.................. John 3:16; Ephesians 2:8–10;
Romans 10:9–13

Sickness.....................James 5:15, 16; Mark 16:17,
18; Jeremiah 33:6; Psalm 41:3; Exodus 15:26

Sin............................1 Corinthians 6:11; 2
Corinthians 5:17; Titus 3:5, 6; Isaiah 1:18; 1 John
1:7; Hebrews 10:22

Temptation.................James 4:7; Romans 8:37; 12:21;
1 Corinthians 10:13; 2 Peter 2:9

Wisdom.................... James 1:5; Psalm 16:7;
Proverbs 9:19; 16:21; Ecclesiastes 2:26; Isaiah 2:3;
1 Corinthians 2:14, 15

O Plano Simples de Deus para a Salvação

Meu amigo!—Faço-te a mais importante pergunta desta vida. Tua alegria ou tristeza por toda a *eternidade* depende dela. Eis a pergunta: estás *salvo*? Não te pergunto se és homem de bem mas estás *salvo*? Ninguem pode gozar das bênções de Deus ou ir para o Céu, sem estar salvo. Jesus disse a Nicomdemus, em *João 3:7*— *"Necessario vos é nascer de novo."* Deus nos deu na Sua Palavra um unico plano de Salvação. Esse plano é simples e, por êle, podes ser salvo—*hoje.*

Primeiro, meu amigo, tens de reconhecer que és pecador. *"Não há justo, nem um sequer."* —*Romanos 3:10. "Porque não há diferença: Todos pecaram e destituidos estão da glória de Deus."*— *Romanos 3:22,23.* Não há oportunidade de seres salvo, se não reconheceres que és pecador.

Porque és pecador e estás condenado a morte! *"Porque o salário do pecado é a morte."—Romanos 6:23. "E o pecado gera a morte."—Tiago 1:15.*

Isto significa separação de Deus, no inferno para sempre. Sim, é terrivel, meu amigo, mas é verdade. Mas Deus te amou tanto que deu Seu Filho unigênito, Jesus Cristo, como teu substituto, para levar teus pecados e morrer em teu lugar. *"Aquele que não conheceu pecado(Jesus) O fez pecado por nós; para que n'Ele fossemos feitos justiça de Deus." —2 Coríntios 5:21. "Levando Ele mesmo em Seu corpo os nossos pecados sobre o madeiro, para que mortos para o pecado, pudessemos viver para a justiça; e pelas Suas feridas fostes sarados."—1 Pedro 2:24.*

Não podemos, agora compreender com os nossos pecados foram colocados sôbre Cristo, mas Deus, em Sua Palavra, diz que foi assim. Assim os teus pecados, meu amigo, foram carregados por Jesus, e Ele morreu em teu lugar. Isto é verdade. Deus não póde mentir!

O carecereiro de Filipos perguntou a Paulo e Silas: Que é necessário que eu faça para me salvar? *"E êles disseram: crê no Senhor Jesus Cristo, e serás salvo, tu e a tua casa."—Atos 16:31.* Basta crer n'Ele como O que carregou teus pecados e morreu no teu lugar. Clama, agora, por Ele!

"Porque todo aquele que invocar o nome do Senhor será salvo."—Romanos 10:13. A primeira oração que um pecador deve fazer, é a seguinte: "O Deus, tem misericórdia de mim, pecador." Agora és um pecador e sentes tristeza por isso. Então, aonde estiveres, podes elevar o teu coração a Deus em oração. Não é necessário fazer uma longa oração em voz alta, porque Deus está ANCIOSO para te salvar. Basta dizeres: "O Deus, sou um pecador arrependido. Tem misericordia de mim e salva me pelo amor de Jesus." Aceita—O, então, diz a Sua Palavra. Romanos 10:13—*"Porque todo aquele (isto te inclui) que invocar o nome do Senhor será salvo, (será salvo, e não talvez seja salvo). Será salvo!*

Crê em Deus e na Sua Palavra. Quando tiveres feito o que Ele te pediu, aceita a salvação pela fé, conforme a Sua Palavra. Crê e serás salvo. Nenhuma igreja, nenhuma sociedade nem as bôas obras—ninguem—mas so e unicamente Jesus Cristo pode te salvar.

O plano simples da Salvação é: és pecador; porque és pecador, deverás morrer ou crer em Cristo que foi teu substituto e morreu em teu lugar. Clama por Ele, reconhecendo que és um pecador e pede—Lhe que tenha misericórdia de ti e te salve, pelo amor de Jesus. Crê, então, na Sua Palavra e, pela fé aceita a salvação. Dirás talvez: "certamente isto não basta para ser salvo." Sim, é—nada mais e absolutamente nada. Graças a Deus, muitas têm sido ganhos para Cristo por êsse simples plano. Está nas Escrituras. E o plano de Deus. Crê n'ele, meu amigo, e SEGUE-O. Agora é o tempo—Hoje é o dia. *"Não presumas do dia de amanhã, porque não sabes o que produzirá o dia."—Provérbios 27:1.* Se não achares perfeitamente claro, lê novamente atê poderes compreender. Não abandones êste folheto, atê que possas entendê-lo totalmente. Tua alma tem mais valor do que tudo mundo.

"Pois que aproveitaria ao homem ganhar todo o mundo e perder a sua alma?"—Marcos 8:36,37, O que daria o homem pelo resgate da sua alma? Não confia nos teus sentimentos. Estes mudam. Firma-te nas promessas de Deus. Estas nunca mudam. Depois que te sentires salvo há três coisas que deves realizar, para o teu crescimento espiritual: *Ora*—e falarás com Deus. Lê a *Biblia*—e Deus falará contigo. *Testifica*—e falarás por Deus.

"Porque Deus amou o mundo de tal maneira que deu o seu Filho unigênito, para que todo aquêle que nêle crê não pereça, mas tenha a vida eterna."—João 3:16

FOR GOD
SO LOVED THE
WORLD THAT HE
GAVE HIS ONE AND
ONLY SON, THAT
WHOEVER BELIEVES
IN HIM SHALL NOT
PERISH BUT HAVE
ETERNAL LIFE.

For God so loved the world
that he gave his one and only Son,
that whoever believes in him
shall not perish but
have eternal life.

—John 3:16

PERSONAL STUDY NOTES

PERSONAL STUDY NOTES

PERSONAL STUDY NOTES

PERSONAL STUDY NOTES

PERSONAL STUDY NOTES

PERSONAL STUDY NOTES

PERSONAL STUDY NOTES

Do your best to
present yourself to God
as one approved, a workman
who does not need to be ashamed
and who correctly handles
the word of truth.
—2 Timothy 2:15